101
ICEBREAKERS

Gary Miller

Heather Horn

ISBN: 978-1-58518-040-0
Library of Congress Control Number: 200792257
Book layout: Deborah Oldenburg
Cover design: Deborah Oldenburg

Healthy Learning
P.O. Box 1828
Monterey, CA 93942
www.healthylearning.com

Dedication

To Kathleen, Erin, and Matthew for your support and patience, and to people willing to venture into places where their comfort levels are challenged.

—G.M.

With love to Gavin, Hudson, and all those seeking the "fun" in every life experience.

—H.H.

Contents

Introduction

The reasons that groups of people are brought together and placed in situations where the individuals interact are many and varied. They may come together as members of an already established organization where a degree of familiarity exists, or they may come without any prior knowledge of the other members of the group. Regardless of the reasons for the gathering of the group or the backgrounds of the individuals present, the development of an open, relaxed atmosphere will enhance the possibilities of learning and positive interaction between the members of the group. The purpose of an icebreaker is to facilitate the development of this atmosphere in which participants can feel comfortable in being part of the group and the exercise at hand. The choice of the icebreaker to be used in the development of the proper atmosphere varies from group to group. Factors that determine the choice include the physical capabilities of the participants, the amount of time available for the icebreaker, the size of the group, and the purpose of the gathering. This book offers the reader a selection of 101 icebreakers designed to enhance the learning potential of any meeting. Choose and enjoy.

1

Short on Time

#1: Challenge Question

Materials: Nerf® Ball

Number of Participants: At least 20 people or more (works well for large groups)

Description: Have the group sit in a circle facing each other, with one person sitting in the center. The ball will be passed around the circle. The person in the middle closes his eyes at the start of the game so he cannot see where the ball is. Tell the person in the center to think of a challenging question that will prompt an individual to name a specified number of things from a certain category. For example, name five foreign cars, seven rivers outside the United States, planets in the Solar System, four flavors of ice cream, etc. When the person in the middle decides on his question he yells, "Stop!" and opens his eyes. The person in the circle who is holding the ball is the one to whom the challenge question is directed.

The center person asks his challenge question. The person with the ball must immediately pass the ball clockwise to the person beside them. Before the ball comes full circle back to them, the challenge question will need to have been answered. If not, that person goes into the middle.

To prevent someone in the center from asking an impossible question (i.e., name 30 dinosaurs) you can allow "The Challenge." When the ball returns to the person answering the question, he can say, "I challenge." The center person must then answer his own question before the ball returns to the start.

Geared Groups: Works best for high school and college age students.

Questions:

- How did teamwork play a role in this activity? Did the group work together or did this generate competition?
- How did this get you ready for the rest of the day?
- Did you learn anything about the personalities of your fellow participants through this activity?

#2: Human Knot

Materials: None

Number of Participants: At least six (when more people are involved, the exercise becomes more difficult)

Description: While standing in a circle, the participants should take their right hands and grasp the right hand of the person directly across the circle from them. Then, they do the same with their left hands, only with a different person. The object is to unscramble the "knot," while still holding hands.

Variations: No verbal communication is allowed, or one pair of hands can be broken to make it easier.

Geared Groups: Works well for groups of all ages.

Questions:

- How did listening play an important role in this activity?
- Did anyone take a leadership role in this activity? How did this contribute to the success of the group?
- How will you use what you learned in this game in other life situations?

#3: Puzzle Challenge

Materials: 60-75 puzzle pieces, plastic storage bags

Number of Participants: Medium to large-size groups

Description: Divide the large group into smaller groups, with each small group at a different table. Evenly distribute the puzzle pieces into the plastic bags so that each table will have a bag with the same number of puzzle pieces. Hand out the bags with the instructions, "Go!" Then, start your watch. Give the entire group approximately 10 minutes to complete the puzzle, counting down aloud to create a pressure situation. Each small group will work only among themselves at their table at the onset of the project, but will soon realize that it is imperative to work with all of the other tables in order to complete the task. The amount of time needed to complete the puzzle and the communication between the groups should be noted for the debriefing.

Geared Groups: Works well with groups of all ages.

Questions:

- Did anyone feel like they were breaking the rules?
- Was there a sense of challenge, like each table was a separate team?
- Some tables emptied quickly. Why do you think this happened, and how did you feel about it?

#4: Team on a Tarp

Materials: A tarp

Number of Participants: At least five, but as the number decreases, make the tarp smaller

Description: Have the entire group stand on the tarp. They must flip the tarp over completely, without anyone stepping off the tarp.

Variations: Limit verbal communication, or only allow certain words.

Geared Groups: Works well with participants who know each other because personal space may be an issue for some people. This game would be fun for all ages.

Questions:

- Were there any strategies that were particularly helpful in allowing your group to be successful?
- Did different leaders emerge at different times during this activity?
- Do you feel more comfortable with the group you are working with now?

#5: Fame

Materials: Paper, pencils

Number of Participants: Medium to large size groups

Description: Have each individual choose a famous person. Each member of the group is given a short period of time to develop the reasons for choosing that person. Everyone is then asked to share the reasons for their choice with the larger group. Allow for duplications of famous people and encourage interaction between the group and the individual as to their reasons for selecting that person.

Variations: Limit the famous person to a particular group such as movie stars or sports personalities.

Geared Groups: Works well for groups of any age.

Questions:

- If the group members know each other: Were there questions from the group regarding the validity of the selection?

- What did the selections reveal about the individual?

- Did any of the selections or reasons surprise the group to the point where they were unable to respond?

#6: I'd Rather Be Called ...

Materials: None

Number of Participants: Medium to large size groups

Description: Create small groups of 5 to 10 individuals. Have each participant introduce himself to the small group using his real name. Then, each member of the group should suggest what he would rather be called. The pseudonym can be a nickname or even a phrase (i.e., man with the plan). An explanation of the name choice and interaction between the group and the individual is expected and should be encouraged.

Variations: Limit the new name to a set of aggressive adjectives such as, "Terminator" or "Chaos."

Geared Groups: Works well for groups of any age.

Questions:

- Did the names selected reveal any new information to the group about an individual?
- Did the names selected differ within the demographics of the group such as age or position within the organization?
- Were nicknames from a previous life experience?

#7: I'm a Star

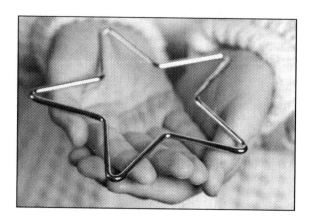

Materials: None

Number of Participants: Medium to large size groups

Description: Each member of the group chooses a movie role that they would like to play and why they chose that role. Allow sufficient time for the members to select their character and develop an explanation as to why they chose that one. Encourage interaction between the presenting individual and the group.

Variations: Allow the individual to change certain aspects of the character to better reflect how they would have played the role.

Geared Groups: Works well for groups high school age or older.

Questions:

- Did the individual take the selected character and all the accompanying characteristics or were they selective as they how they viewed the character?
- Did others in the group view the same character differently?
- Were all of the characters selected the "star" of the film or did some members select "supporting" actors?

#8: What's on a Penny?

Materials: A penny, paper, pencils

Number of Participants: At least six to nine people to allow for three groups of two to three

Description: Separate people into groups of equal numbers. Determine the sufficient time limit for this activity and instruct the groups to write down as many things as they can remember that are on the penny in the time allotted.

Geared Groups: Works well with groups of every age.

Questions:

• How did this game lead you to work with other people?

• Were there consistencies in the lists and why might those items have been noticed more so than other defining characteristics of the penny?

• Were they any glaring omissions in your group's list?

#9: Moving Day

Materials: Anything that can be used to mark locations on the floor

Number of Participants: Small groups

Description: Arrange the participants in a circle with markers on the floor for all but one of the participants to stand. The person without a spot stands in the middle of the group and asks a yes/no question such as, "Were you born east of the Mississippi River?" All those people who can answer "yes" to the question have to move to another spot in the circle that is not directly adjacent to the one they are currently occupying by going across the center of the circle. The person who does not get to a spot before it is occupied by another member of the group is the new person in the middle and asks a new question.

Geared Groups: Works well for high school age groups or older.

Questions:

- Did the group discover something new about each other?
- Did some members of the group quickly understand the strategy of asking a question that possibly only one person could answer in the affirmative?
- Did the game get physical and competitive?

#10: It's Not My Job

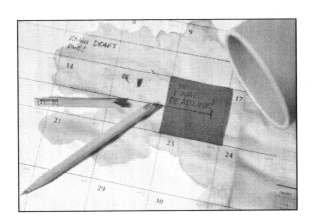

Materials: Paper, pencils

Number of Participants: Any number

Description: On a piece of paper, each member of the group writes down the strangest job or task within a job they have ever held or done. Following an appropriate length of time—it shouldn't take very long—the group reconvenes and each member shares his job with the group. Encourage discussion and details regarding the circumstances of the job including how long they stayed with the job.

Variations: Have each person write down three strange jobs, two that they did not perform and one they did. Have the group decide which of the three jobs the person actually performed.

Geared Groups: Works well for high-school-age groups or older.

Questions:

- Did the group discover something new about its members?
- Was the exercise fun for the group?
- Did the exercise reveal that members of the group come from different backgrounds and experiences?

#11: That's Odd

Materials: Paper, pencils

Number of Participants: Any number

Description: Each member of the group writes on a piece of paper one or two things about themselves that they feel other members of the group may consider to be odd. Following an appropriate amount of time for development, reconvene the group and have each member share his "oddities" with the group.

Variations: Have the members list their oddities with their names and have the leader read them to the group without the name identification. Let the group guess whose oddity is whose.

Geared Groups: Works well for older aged groups.

Questions:

- Did the group discover anything new about its members?
- Did the members of the group readily share their peculiarities?
- Did anyone not participate in this activity? If not, why?

#12: Texas Hold 'Em

Materials: Enough cards for every person to have two cards, five cards for the center, a progressive list of winning poker hands

Number of Participants: Medium size groups

Description: Two cards are distributed to each member of the group. Three cards (the flop) are placed face up in the center of the room so all members of the group can see them plainly. The group is then asked to line up in ascending (or descending) order according to the poker hand they can form using their two cards and the flop. Then, a fourth card (the turn card) is added to the flop in the center and the group is asked to reposition themselves according to the new hands they can form using their two cards and the four cards in the center. Finally, a fifth card (the river card) is added to the flop and the turn card. The group is then asked to reposition themselves according to their final hands–five cards constitute a hand. They can assemble using their two cards and the five cards available in the center of the room.

Variations: Institute a time limit for positioning themselves and remove anyone who is out of position from the exercise.

Geared Groups: Works well with high-school-age groups or older.

Questions:

- Was it easy to illustrate how the changing cards are similar to changing factors that affect other positions?
- How did the group handle identical hands in the positioning role?
- Were the individuals unfamiliar with the game of poker at a distinct disadvantage?

#13: Count the F's

Materials: Card or sheet of paper (see Figure 13-1)

Number of Participants: 15 to 20 people

Description: To illustrate that people see what they want to see, pass out facedown copies of the page shown in Figure 13-1. When everyone is ready, ask them to turn the paper over and simply count how many times the letter "f" appears on their sheet. Allow only a minute, and then ask, "How many of you have the sheet with the three F's?" (Roughly half the group can be expected to raise their hands.) Then ask, "Who has four F's on their sheet? ... How about five? ... Does anyone have six?" (About 50% of the group will see only three F's, and approximately 10% will see all six F's. The rest will see either four or five on the sheet.)

Variations: Ask those with four, five, or six F's on their sheets to raise their hands and let those with three F's to exchange papers so they too can "see" all six F's. Most will still have a difficult time identifying all six of the F's.

Geared Groups: Works best with high-school-age groups and older.

Questions:

- Why couldn't all of us initially see all six F's? (The F in the word "of" sounds like a "V".)

- Have you observed situations where only the important things get attention? Who decides what's important?

- How can we persuade people to pay more attention to details? Is it always important?

Count the F's

FEATURE FILMS ARE THE RE-

SULT OF YEARS OF SCIENTI-

FIC STUDY COMBINED WITH

THE EXPERIENCE OF YEARS

Figure 13-1

#14: Movie Ball

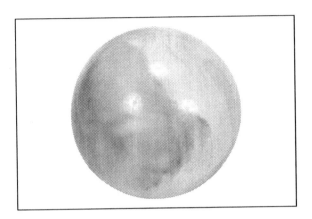

Materials: One ball that bounces

Number of Participants: Medium to large size groups

Description: Organize everyone in a circle. Give one person a ball and instruct him to start by saying a title of a movie. He must bounce the ball to another person within five seconds. The person he bounces the ball to must either: a) name another movie (normal play) or b) name a movie in which an actor from the previously named movie also acted in (challenge play). Example: If player A says, "Top Gun" then player B can say, "Risky Business." The second player then bounces the ball to another player and the game continues. When someone repeats a movie name, that player is out. It will eventually come down to two players, and the winner is given a prize (optional).

Geared Groups: Works best with all ages.

Questions:

- How did this warm-up activity prepare you for the rest of the day?
- What did you learn from working together as a team?
- Did this activity begin to make you feel comfortable with those individuals you will be working with for the rest of the day?

#15: I'm Feeling Faint

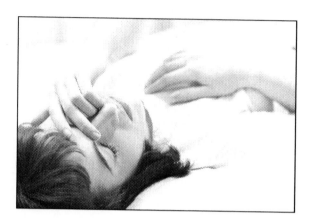

Materials: Paper, pencils

Number of Participants: Any number

Description: Each person in the group is asked to write on a piece paper those things that they "hate to see." Provide only the guide phrase, "hate to see." Part of the exercise is to determine how different people will interpret what the phrase means to them, thus emphasizing the importance and necessity of clear communication within the organization. Each member then presents to the larger group their items and why they hate to see those things.

Geared Groups: Works well with any age group.

Questions:

- Did some of the group think of the phrase as meaning physically repulsive items?
- How did people interpret the meaning of this activity differently?
- Was the process easy or difficult?

2

Minimum Materials Needed

#16: The Librarian

Materials: 3" x 5" index cards

Number of Participants: Between 5 and 20 people

Description: Participants place their names at the top of an index card. Each participant lists the three most important books they have ever read. Participants are paired and asked to share why these books were important to them.

Variations: Restrict the book choices to fiction/nonfiction or work-related/pleasure reading.

Geared Groups: Works best for high school to college ages.

Questions:

- What did you learn about your partner in this exercise?
- Did you learn something about your partner that you did not previously know?
- What role did communication play?

#17: Remember Me

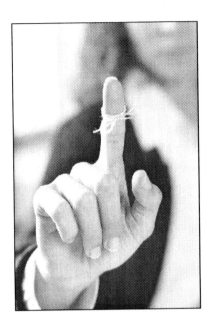

Materials: 3" x 5" index cards

Number of Participants: Between 5 and 20 people

Description: Participants place their names at the top of an index card. Each participant then writes down those things they would hope people would remember about them after they are gone. Leave the process as open as possible—allow participants to write whatever they wish, from basic facts (e.g., birth dates, death dates, hometowns, etc.) to accomplishments of their life's work. Their style is as telling as the content! Have each person read his card to the group or exchange and have another person read the card. Allow time for questions from the group.

Variations: Restrict the items listed to only those accomplishments outside of the workplace or only those things done with their present employer/organization.

Geared Groups: Works best for high school to college ages.

Questions:

- What did the group learn about its members in this exercise?
- Did the group learn something about the styles preferred by each individual?
- How did the questions from the group change the focus of communication?

#18: True or False

Materials: Paper, pencils

Number of Participants: At least 20 to 30

Description: Each member of the group is given a sheet of paper on which to write down three items about themselves that they consider to be interesting or unique. Two of the items must be true and one must be false. Each member is asked to share his list with the group and the group must decide which statement is false. No questions are allowed to the individual reading his list. Decisions must be made by the group based solely upon the statement as presented.

Geared Groups: Almost any age group, but works best with high-school-age participants and older.

Variations: Switch the mix of the statements so that only one statement is true and the group must determine which statement is true.

Questions:

- How will this information benefit your group development?
- Were members willing to openly share their lists?
- What were some of the believable statements? If you did this activity again, what would you change to make your statement(s) more believable?

#19: When I Was Young

Materials: Paper, pencils

Number of Participants: Any number

Description: Each participant should list five notable things from their childhood. These can be events relating to family, school memories (i.e., first day, best teacher, etc.), or the cost of goods and services during that time versus today. Allow the participants latitude in developing what their lists contain. Re-form the group and have each individual share selected items or their entire list depending upon the size of the group and time available.

Variations: Limit the contents of the list to specific information such as high school years or working career

Geared Groups: Works well for groups of all ages.

Questions:

- Were there distinguishable differences between genders or age groups?
- Was there a general willingness to share information?
- What did the group learn about its individual members?

#20: The First Time

Materials: Paper, pencils

Number of Participants: Larger groups

Description: Working individually, each participant should list three "firsts" in their lives (i.e., first job, first day of school, first pet, or any other significant event in their lives). Reconvene the group and have each individual share his list with the group. Provide enough time for individuals to explain the significance of the event they are sharing.

Variations: Limit the "first" to specific time periods or work-related events.

Geared Groups: Works well with college-age groups and older.

Questions:

- Were the "firsts" grouped in a specific manner?
- Did some individuals have a difficult time developing the list?
- Were the "firsts" more career-oriented or personal?

#21: It Looks Like Rain

Materials: Paper, pencils

Number of Participants: Medium to large groups

Description: Pair participants into groups of two and have each person work independently. Each person lists those areas in their work life that are going well and how a "shower of rain" would negatively affect that area. Then, each person lists those areas in their work life where a "shower of rain" would allow them to grow and improve their performance. The paired groups should spend a couple of minutes discussing their lists and each participant should choose one example to explain to the whole group. After the pairs discussion, reconvene the entire group and have all the group members share their examples

Variations: Reconvene the groups according to work units rather than across the entire work organization.

Geared Groups: Works well with groups of all ages.

Questions:

- How did your group respond to the revelations of the group members?
- Were the negative effects of "rain" something that the organization can readily address?
- Were the negative effects of rain more pronounced than the positive effects of rain?

#22: AKA (Also Known As)

Materials: Card stock paper (4″ x 6″ or larger), markers

Number of Participants: Small to medium size groups

Description: Every organization has its share of acronyms and names for buildings, programs, or services. Divide the participants into small groups and have each small group choose one or two examples from a prepared list and develop alternatives for those acronyms and names. For example, CIA could also stand for "Certainly Incompetent Agency."

Variations: Have the individuals work only on organizational names and acronyms within the work unit.

Geared Groups: Works well with high school groups or older.

Questions:

- Did your group respond with creative and clever new ideas?
- Were the new names positive in nature or negative?
- Did the new acronyms and names reflect a perception on the part of your clientele or your employees?

#23: If I Could Go Back

Materials: Paper, pencils

Number of Participants: Medium to large-size groups

Description: Divide the group into pairs. Working independently, each person lists things they wish they could go back and do again. Do not give direction or any restriction on the type of situation that could be listed. Each person then shares one or more of his items with his partner. Reconvene the larger group and have each member share one of his items with the group.

Variations: Concentrate on impersonal decisions only.

Geared Groups: Works well with high-school-age participants and older.

Questions:

- What new information did the group discover about individuals?
- Were members of the group willing to share both work-related and personal decisions?
- Were most of the items listed work-related or personal?

#24: Take Out an Ad

Materials: Paper, pencils

Number of Participants: Any size group

Description: Have each individual write a want ad soliciting the perfect employee. The ad should be a rudimentary job description, work hours, and salary. Leave any additional qualifications to the discretion of the individual. Reconvene the group and have each member read his ad. See if the group can create a single ad for the perfect employee.

Variations: Limit the ad to a specific position or area within the organization.

Geared Groups: Works well with high-school-age participants and older.

Questions:

- Were the ads realistic or were they unattainable?
- Did the job qualifications beyond the basics reflect the feelings of the developer?
- Was the group able to reach any consensus on the development of an overall perfect employee ad?

#25: Wanna Play?

Materials: Paper, pencils, list of children's games

Number of Participants: Medium to large size groups

Description: Divide the group into smaller subgroups of three to five people. Assign a children's game to each group with the instructions that they are to modify the game and improve it. Do not restrict the creativity of the small groups by giving them too many directions. After an appropriate amount of time, each group presents their new game to the rest of the larger group. Allow for explanations and even demonstrations of how to play the new game. Encourage additional ideas from the group on other improvements.

Variations: Give every group the same game and assess how the different groups attacked the problem.

Geared Groups: Works well for any age group.

Questions:

- Did one member of the subgroup take the lead and shape the changes made to the assigned game?
- Did any member of any subgroup not participate?
- Did the subgroup exhaust all of the possible improvements to the game?
- How did the group present their enhancements to the game: demonstration or verbal? Why do you think some groups chose to demonstrate their changes while other groups chose to verbally communicate their enhancements? What might this tell about a group?

#26: It's a Mystery to Me

Materials: 3" x 5" index card, pencils

Number of Participants: Small to medium size groups

Description: Each member of the group takes an index card and writes three unique statements about themselves on the card (two items that are true and one that is false) without their name or any other identifying information. The cards are collected and read aloud. From the items on the card the group must guess who wrote the card and which of the three items is false.

Variations: Change from having two things true to only having one item be true.

Geared Groups: Works well for high-school-age groups or older.

Questions:

- Did the group learn something new about the individual members?
- What was the most unique "true" statement?
- What was the most unique "false" statement?

#27: Jingles

Materials: Paper, pencils

Number of Participants: Any number

Description: Have each member of the group write down on a piece of paper an advertising slogan or line from a song that represents his position within the group. Each member then explains his selection to the larger group. Encourage discussion between the presenting member and the members of the group.

Variations: Have subgroups of the organization meet as a group to make a selection for their area.

Geared Groups: Works well for any age group.

Questions:

- Did the slogan or lines chosen illustrate a difference based on age of the member?
- Did the explanations for the selection stimulate discussions between the member and the remaining members of the group?
- Were most of the slogans or lines designed to be humorous?

#28: Letters From Home

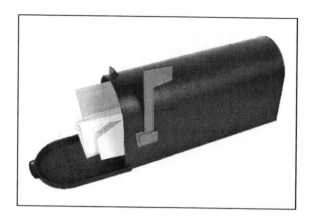

Materials: Paper, pencils

Number of Participants: Medium to large groups

Description: Have each member of the group write down on a piece of paper the type and frequency of emotional support they feel is most important in the daily completion of his work. Each member then shares his information with the group. Encourage discussion between the member sharing his information and the larger group.

Geared Groups: Works well for high-school-age groups or older.

Questions:

- Were the members readily able to share their emotional needs without reservations?
- Did the selections stimulate discussions between the member and the remaining members of the group?
- Did any member of the group refuse to share his emotional needs with the group?

#29: You're Hired

Materials: Paper, pencils

Number of Participants: Medium to large size groups

Description: Have each member of the group write down on a piece of paper a press release to the local newspaper announcing his hiring with the organization. Provide some direction to the members of the group with the fact that most announcements would include name, date of hire, and title/job responsibilities, but leave any other embellishments or inclusions to the discretion of the author. Each member then shares his announcement with the larger group.

Variations: Have the members pair up and write the hiring announcement for their partner.

Geared Groups: Works well for any age group.

Questions:

- Did the group discover something new about its members?
- Which members of the group kept their announcement to the basics and which members expanded upon them?
- What were some of the most frequently mentioned embellishments?

#30: And the Winner Is ...

Materials: 3" x 5" index cards, pencils

Number of Participants: Medium to large size groups

Description: Make sure everyone has an index card and a pencil. Working independently, have each person describe in written detail a "winning" moment in their lives. The moment can be group related or personal, but should include all of the circumstances of why the individual feels that his was a winning moment for them. Each person then shares his winning moment with the larger group.

Variations: Limit the winning moments to those that have occurred in their working career.

Geared Groups: Works well for high-school-age or older groups.

Questions:

• Were more winning moments from things inside the organization or from personal moments?

• Did the exercise reveal any new information about the members?

• How was winning defined differently from individual to individual?

#31: The Good, the Bad, Without the Ugly

Materials: Post-it® sheets for the wall, markers

Number of Participants: Any number

Description: Divide the group into subgroups of three to five members. Have each group work on employee traits that fall into one category–good or the other category–bad. Have the subgroups make the lists as extensive and inclusive as possible. Allow for sufficient time for the development of the lists. Post each group's list on the wall, eliminate duplications and discuss the composite lists among all the members of the larger group.

Geared Groups: Works well for high-school-age groups or older.

Questions:

- Was the good list or bad list longer?
- Did the same quality appear on both lists?
- Was an item listed on the good list by one group and the bad list by another?
- Did this generate a constructive discussion?

#32: It's a Zoo

Materials: None

Number of Participants: Any number

Description: Each member of the group chooses an animal commonly found in a zoo. Following the choice, each member explains what life is like for this animal in its zoo location. Encourage participants to reveal feelings about being on constant display, role expectations of being this animal and in a zoo, and the different types of interactions that occur on a regular basis as a part of being this animal. The point of this exercise is to investigate the comfort level of each individual as they function as a part of the overall team.

Variations: A simpler version would just allow the group members to explain why any visitor to the zoo would want to come and see them as the animal they chose.

Geared Groups: Works well with high-school-age groups or older.

Questions:

- Was revealing their feelings easier for some than it was for others?
- How did different "animals" feel about being on display and having to play a role?
- Did group members who were reluctant to share their feelings loosen up as others went through the exercise?

#33: Everybody Up

Materials: None

Number of Participants: Medium to large size groups

Description: Have the group pair up with someone who is around their same height and weight. Have them sit on the ground facing that person, with the soles of their shoes touching. They are to reach out and grab their partner's hands and pull as hard as they can. They are trying to pull each other up into a standing position. Participants can communicate to find the best way to do this. Once they have completed that, have them change their partners to a less similar body type.

Geared Groups: 14- to 18-year-olds who do not know each other.

Questions:

- Would this work well with older individuals?
- Was the reason for pairing up with similar body types evident in the first part of the exercise?
- Was the reason for changing to a partner with a different body type just as evident?
- Did you and your partner implement any useful strategies?

3

Getting Comfortable

#34: Ball Frantic

Materials: Balloons, beach balls, Koosh® balls

Number of Participants: Between 7 and 20 people

Description: Participants gather in a circle, throw the balls in the air, and try to keep them there for as long as possible.

Variations: Restrict the use of certain body parts (example: only heads or feet may touch the balls), or add extra balls to make it more difficult.

Geared Groups: Works best for high school to college-age groups.

Questions:

- Did this activity get you ready for the rest of the day's activities?
- How did the team work together while participating in this activity?
- What unique communication strategy did your group utilize? Was it successful?

#35: Bunny, Bunny

Materials: None

Number of Participants: Groups of seven or more

Description: Participants gather in a circle. Select one person to be the "bunny." He immediately bends down, with hands on knees and says, "Bunny, bunny, bunny, bunny, bunny, bunny, bunny." While the selected participant is reciting these words, the individuals to both his right and left begin forming the ears of the bunny with their left or right arm, depending on their position. They will also join in the "bunny" chant. On the seventh repetition, the selected individual will then point to another person in the circle and send "bunny" off to that participant. If the "bunny" or either of the "ears" (the individuals to the right and left) do not play their part or do it incorrectly, then they are eliminated. This fast-paced activity continues until all but two participants are eliminated for neglecting to do their part of the job.

Variations: In addition to "bunny," other actions can be incorporated into the game to make it more challenging. These include: "Charlie's Angels," which involves the words, "Boom chika, boom chika, boom chika," with accompanied hands raising imaginary guns in the air—straight up, in the center, and to the left or right, depending on the individual's side; and "pony" which involves the three individuals chanting, "Pony, pony, pony, pony, pony, pony, pony," while the one in the middle acts like they are riding a horse, and the two on the sides follow this same motion or turn a lasso.

Geared Groups: Works well and is fun for all age groups!

Questions:

- Did this exercise get you warmed up and ready for the day?
- Do you now feel more comfortable with the group that you will be working with for the next couple of hours?
- What do you think was the key message of this game? How is this lesson important in activities like this one, as well as in everyday life?

#36: Chair Sit

Materials: None

Number of Participants: At least five people, but the larger the group, the better

Description: Have players form a line or a circle, with each individual being somewhat close to the person in front of them. Have them begin walking in their formation while singing a silly song that you give to them. At any random time, interrupt their song and tell them to sit. If done correctly and at the same time, they will all end up sitting in the lap of the person directly behind them. However, if they do not all trust to sit at the same time, everyone playing will fall to the ground. If the group masters this task, have them walk while sitting.

Geared Groups: Works well for groups who do not know each other well. It is also fun for all age groups, but high school and college students may enjoy it the most.

Questions:

- Did your group trust one another?
- Was there a way you could have succeeded more quickly?
- How can you apply this activity to everyday life?

#37: Fire in the Hole

Materials: Blown-up balloons

Number of Participants: Nine or more

Description: Divide into groups of three to five participants and give each group three to five balloons (one balloon per participant). Each participant places a balloon between himself and a partner, halfway between the base of the neck and the naval, just below the breastbone. Have the group form a small circle, put their arms around each other, and prepare to squeeze to pop the balloons. Before they squeeze, have them shout, "Fire in the hole!" to warn the bystanders of the impending blow.

Geared Groups: Works best with high school-aged students.

Questions:

- How did this warm-up activity prepare you for the rest of the day?
- What did you learn from working together as a team?
- Did "personal space" issues come into play?

#38: Flip Me the Bird

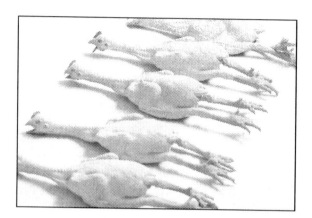

Materials: Rubber chicken or a similar item (use two or more items if the game has more than 20 participants)

Number of Participants: 10 or more

Description: One person is given the rubber chicken. Another person is designated as "it." The person who is "it" runs around and tries to tag another person. If he is successful, the person tagged becomes "it." Whoever is holding the rubber chicken has immunity and cannot be tagged. If a free person is being chased, they can call out, "Flip me the bird!," and if someone throws them a rubber chicken before they are tagged, they are safe. The game concludes when all participants have been tagged without the immunity of the rubber chicken.

Geared Groups: Works best with high school to college-age individuals.

Questions:

- Did this activity foster teamwork or competition among self-defined groups?
- How did this warm-up activity prepare you for the rest of the day?
- Was the person who had immunity willing to share the rubber chicken?

#39: Oh Baby!

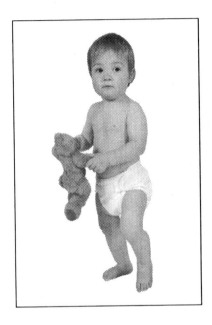

Materials: Baby picture from each individual, paper, pencils

Number of Participants: Works well with medium-sized groups

Description: Each participant's photo is displayed on a wall with only a number identification. All participants are asked to identify the adult group member with one of the photos on the wall. Upon identification each member is asked to share one defining quality they had when they were a child and whether or not that quality has changed over the passage of time.

Geared Groups: Works well with most groups.

Questions:

- How have people changed or how do people believe they have changed over time?
- Was this a fun activity that allowed some members of the group to let down their guard?
- Which individual changed the most and which stayed the same?

#40: The Joker

Materials: Jokes without captions

Number of Participants: Medium to large-size groups

Description: Post a number of jokes on the wall without any captions. Have participants work individually or in small groups to create the captions for the jokes. Allow participants full latitude to offer any possible caption.

Variations: Limit the caption responses to a specified number of words or sentences.

Geared Groups: Works well for groups of high school age and older.

Questions:

- Did everyone see the same situation in the jokes?
- Did certain jokes lend themselves to a single perception among the members of the group?
- Did anyone have a unique perception for any of the jokes?

#41: Trip to the Farm

Materials: Blindfolds

Number of Participants: 10 or more people (number must be even); works best with a large group

Description: Quietly give the name of one animal to each of the participants, making sure that pairs of people will have the same animal. Distribute the blindfolds to the individuals, and instruct them to find their match only by using the sounds that their particular animal would use.

Geared Groups: Works well with groups of every age, but especially good with younger participants.

Questions:

- How did this game lead you to work with other people?
- Did differing interpretations of animal sounds make it difficult to find your pair?
- How did this warm-up activity prepare you for the rest of the day?

#42: Vacation

Materials: Paper, markers

Number of Participants: Any size group works well as long as smaller groups of three to seven can be made.

Description: Split the group into subgroups of three to seven participants. Explain that they are to work together to produce what an ideal vacation would include. They can use words, symbols, and drawings in creating their vacation scenario. Allow for time for the groups to explain their products at the end.

Variations: Instead of a vacation, have the groups describe their ideal house. The topic can also be changed by the facilitator as well.

Geared Groups: For college-age groups and older.

Questions:

- Did this activity help you get ready for the rest of the day?
- Were separate vacations made or did the group plan a vacation for all of them to travel on together?
- Did the group experience any difficulties in coming to a consensus if they traveled together?

#43: You Tear Me Up

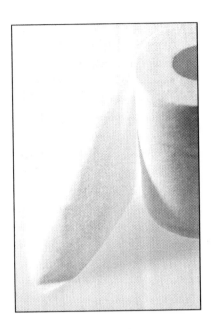

Materials: A roll of toilet paper

Number of Participants: Any number

Description: Without further explanation, pass a roll of toilet paper around the room and tell participants to rip off as many sheets as they would like. When the roll has gone all the way around the room, tell them that they have to tell the group one thing about themselves for each sheet of toilet paper that they have. Allow a minute for them to gather their thoughts, and then, starting at the front of the room, work your way around until everyone has told a little about themselves.

Geared Groups: Works well with groups of every age.

Questions:

- Did you discover something new about your fellow participants?
- How did this activity prepare you for the rest of the program?
- How can this activity apply to everyday life (i.e., work, school, etc)?

#44: Protecting Your Dreams

Materials: 3" x 5" index card, pencils

Number of Participants: Small to medium size groups

Description: Each member of the group takes an index card and writes just one of their dreams/ambitions on the card. Place all of the completed cards on a table face down. Announce that you will be sharing *some* of the dreams with the group. Looking at each card, read some of the cards aloud and discard others until the stack of cards is exhausted. Discuss with the group how they felt when their dream was read and how they felt when their dream was not read.

Variations: Ask that the dreams be directly related to the group or organizational goals.

Geared Groups: Works well for high-school-age groups or older.

Questions:

*   Were any of the members of the group emotionally devastated when their dream was not read?
*   Was there any empathy for those members whose dreams were not read?
*   Was the leader of the group perceived to have some legitimate power because of their ability to read or not read someone's dream?

#45: Complete the Thought

Materials: 3" x 5" index card, pencils, index cards with parts of famous quotes written on them

Number of Participants: Any number

Description: Each member of the group takes an index card that contains part of a famous quote. Working independently, the members of the group are asked to complete the quote. For example, a partial quote could be, "A bird in the hand…" The members share their completed quotes with the group. Encourage dialog between the group and the presenting individual for alternative answers.

Variations: Use partial nursery rhymes.

Geared Groups: Works well for high-school-age groups or older.

Questions:

- Were most of the answers directed toward humor?
- Were any of the new quotes deemed to be better than the original?
- Did the group members have fun with this exercise?

#46: Plants Have Feelings Too

Materials: Paper, pencils

Number of Participants: Any number

Description: Ask each member of the group to choose a plant and list the attributes that most closely fit with their personality. Each choice and list is shared with the group. Encourage discussion from the group regarding the individual's choice and list of attributes.

Variations: Limit the choices to agricultural crops or flowers only.

Geared Groups: Works well for any age group.

Questions:

- Did anyone choose an incredibly outrageous plant that created a lot of discussion?
- Did any particular plant dominate the selection process?
- Did the group members have fun with this exercise?

#47: In Order, Please

Materials: Props to throw such as stuffed animals

Number of Participants: Small groups

Description: Place the members of the group in a circle facing one another. Give each member of the group a prop (i.e., stuffed animal, Nerf® ball, etc). The leader of the group begins by calling out the name of the prop he is holding and the name of the prop held by the person to whom he is tossing. For example, "bear" to "dog." The person with the dog catches the bear and calls out another prop name, then tosses the dog to the person holding that prop. The exchange of props continues until everyone has passed their prop to another person. The object is to accomplish one repetition in the same order with ever-increasing speed.

Variations: Have more than one prop moving around the circle at a time.

Geared Groups: Works well for any age group.

Questions:

- Did the members work together as a team to increase the speed and efficiency?
- Were people able to easily follow the sequence of the exchange of props?
- Were any of the group members frustrated with the performance of other members?

#48: When I Grow Up

Materials: Paper, pencil

Number of Participants: Any number

Description: Have each member of the group assume that they are six-years-old and then, write on a piece of paper what they want to be when they grow up. Each choice should contain some explanation of why the choice was made. Reconvene the group and have each member share his aspirations with the group.

Variations: Ask the members to write their aspirations and the reasons why they had changed.

Geared Groups: Works well for high-school-age groups and older.

Questions:

- Did anyone in the group actually achieve what he had aspired to be at the age of six?
- Were the choices realistic or more influenced by the childhood events and environment?
- Was one influence of choice or change more prominently mentioned than another?

#49: A Bad Deal

Materials: Enough playing cards to deal each person five cards, a list of progressively better poker hands

Number of Participants: Small groups

Description: Each member of the group receives five playing cards upon entering the room. After everyone has arrived, explain that just like in poker not every hand is a "good hand." Allow everyone to analyze their hands noting the positive aspects of any one card and the negative aspects of the same card. Finally, the member is asked to analyze the positive and negative aspects of the five cards as a group. Each member shares his hand and its positives and negatives with the larger group.

Variations: Have the members trade certain cards in a "group trading session" in order to improve their own hand.

Geared Groups: Works well for older age groups.

Questions:

- Did the group discover anything new about its members?
- Were members of the group able to see the positive aspects of even the worst cards?
- Could the group make the transition from the cards to factors they have been "dealt" in their lives?

#50: Fruits and Nuts

Materials: 3" x 5" index cards, pencils

Number of Participants: Medium to large size groups

Description: Working independently, have each person give a written description about himself as indicated by a fruit or nut. Each selection must be accompanied by an explanation as to why that fruit or nut was chosen. Each member shares his selection with the larger group.

Variations: Try any other agricultural commodity.

Geared Groups: Works well for any age group.

Questions:

- What positive characteristics were most prominently assigned to the chosen fruit or nut?
- Were there exotic selections or did people stick with traditional fruits and nuts?
- Was there one explanation that changed your perception of a person?

#51: Wrestling

Paul Hawthorne/Getty Images

Materials: 3" x 5" index cards, pencils

Number of Participants: Medium to large size groups

Description: Working independently, have each person create for himself a nickname that could be given to any professional wrestler. Give as little direction as possible for this exercise to allow the people as much latitude as possible. Suggest that they use something that is descriptive or "marketable" for themselves. Provide potential examples such as: Frank "Good Night" Knight, or David "Gold" Rusch. Allow time for everyone to share their names with the larger group.

Variations: Have pairs of individuals supply the names for their partners.

Geared Groups: Works well for any age group.

Questions:

- Do you think any of these new nicknames will stick with the individual?
- Did the exercise loosen the group up for the point of the meeting?
- Was everyone able to think up a name that was descriptive and reflective of their personality?

#52: Listening Exercise

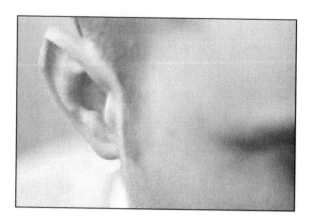

Materials: Any newspaper article with several facts contained therein, a prepared list of questions regarding the article

Number of Participants: Small to medium size groups—ideally 10 to 25 participants

Description: To demonstrate that most adults listen at about a 25% level of efficiency, clip a story from a newspaper or magazine that is approximately two or three paragraphs long. With absolutely no introduction, casually mention to your group, "... some of you probably saw the item in the paper the other day," and read aloud the entire two to three paragraphs. When finished, you'll see a room of either bored or disinterested faces. Pull out a dollar bill and state, "Ok, I've got a few questions for you based on the story you just heard, and whoever gets them all right wins this dollar." Read 8 to 10 prepared questions (i.e., names, dates, places, etc.). In all likelihood, not one person will be able to answer *all* questions correctly.

Geared Groups: Works best with college-age individuals and older.

Questions:

- You all heard that story, yet few could remember very much about it. Why? (i.e., disinterest, no objective, no advance reward, etc.)

- Why didn't we listen? Is this typical? What can we do to sharpen our listening skills?

- If I had told you initially you could win some money, would you have listened more attentively? Why? How can we ensure better listening (without monetary rewards)?

#53: Following Oral Directions

Materials: List of mathematical problems (see Figure 53-1)

Number of Participants: Small to medium size groups—ideally 10 to 25 participants

Description: To illustrate the difficulty of attentive listening, ask the group to take a sheet of blank paper and number it from 1 to 15. They are to listen carefully to each question and do all calculations mentally, writing *only* the answers down on the paper. Read the questions found on the following page at the normal rate of speech.

Geared Groups: Works best with college-age individuals and older.

Questions:

- How many of us just quit listening when we got confused or "lost" with a question?
- Have you seen times when people seem to tune you out when you're giving instructions?
- What can we do to prevent this loss of attention or to encourage active listening?

Procedure:

1. Start with 8; double it; add 4; divide by 5; the answer is _____.
2. Start with 11; subtract 3; add 4; add 3; divide by 3; the answer is _____.
3. Start with 15; add 10; divide by 5; multiply by 6; add 6; divide by 4; the answer is _____.
4. From a number that is 4 larger than 13, add 5; divide by 2; subtract 3; the answer is _____.
5. From a number that is 2 smaller than 9, add 6; add 5; multiply by 2; divide by 4; the answer is _____.
6. Add 6 to 12; subtract 9; add 10; subtract 13; double it; the answer is _____.
7. Add 4 to 5; add 6; add 7; add 9; add 9; divide by 4; the answer is _____.
8. Subtract 6 from 11; add 5; multiply by 5; subtract 15; subtract 10; add 1; the answer is _____.
9. From a number that is larger than 6, add 3; divide by 5; multiple by 4; add 1; the answer is _____.
10. Take the square root of 36; add5; add 14; divide by 5; add 3; divide by 4; the answer is _____.
11. From a number that is 5 larger than 6, subtract 3; add 2; add 3; divide by 4; the answer is _____.
12. In the series of numbers, 4-7-8-6-9-12, the first three numbers were _____.
13. In the series of numbers, 4-6-9-9-7-6-3, the sum of the first three numbers is _____.
14. In the series of numbers, 7-9-6-8-4-9-6-10, the lowest odd number is _____.
15. In the series of numbers, 4-5-7-8-6-2-1-9, the sum of these numbers is _____.

Answers:

(1) 4; (2) 5; (3) 9; (4) 8; (5) 9; (6) 12; (7) 10; (8) 26; (9) 13; (10) 2; (11) 11; (12) 4-7-8; (13) 19; (14) 7; (15) 42.

Figure 53-1

#54: Memory

Materials: None

Number of Participants: Any number, but the more people you have, the more fun

Description: Organize everyone in a circle. One person begins by performing an action (i.e., patting his head). The person to his left must repeat the action, and add another action. The game progresses with each person having to repeat all the previous actions in order, then adding one. If a player misses an action or fouls up, that player is out. The game can continue for as many rounds as time allows.

Geared Groups: Fun for all ages.

Questions:

- At what point did you reach your ability to perform all of the actions?
- Did this activity frustrate or motivate you?

#55: Picture Portrait

Materials: A white board, white board markers and erasers

Number of Participants: Small to medium size groups

Description: Ask each participant to come up to the white board and express something about themselves, not verbally, but through a series of drawings. Come up with three or four topics about the participants you would like for everyone to share (i.e., first name, hobby, pet peeve, favorite food.) After each participant finishes drawing, the other participants will try and guess the right interpretations. The person at the board can give additional clues, but only through more drawings. Each participant takes a turn until everyone has introduced himself.

Geared Groups: Works best for grammar school through college-age groups

Questions:

- Did the group learn something new about its members?
- Was this a non-threatening, fun way to introduce themselves?

4

Engaging the Masses:
Extra-Large Groups

#56: I'm From...

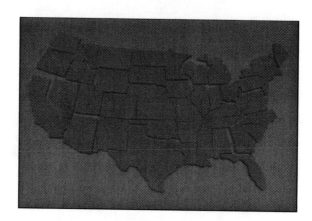

Materials: None

Number of Participants: From 10 to 30 people, but could accommodate larger numbers

Description: Divide a geographic area into three parts. You can use the world, the country, the state, or a city, depending upon the diversity of the group. Each group is formed and gathers to spend time discussing the unique aspects of their geographic area. The groups should list attractions to living in their area as well as detractions. Following a development period, a spokesperson from each group presents its "case" for their area being the best place to be from. Allow time for questions from the group and permit all individuals from the questioned group to answer, rather than just the spokesperson.

Variations: Use different descriptors such as population of hometown or number of children in the family.

Geared Groups: Works well for groups who do not know each other well. It is also fun for all age groups, but high school and college students may enjoy it the most.

Questions:

- Was there any particular phrase (i.e., soda or pop) used in one geographic area more frequently than another?

- Was the process divisive or did it bring people closer?

- Was each group accepting of differences or competitive to be the best?

#57: Getting to Know You

Materials: Pencils, chart of different characteristics/experiences (such as color of hair, height, birthplace, college years, generational differences, career choices)

Number of Participants: Groups of 20 or more

Description: Distribute a chart to each participant along with a pencil. Tell them to find an individual who matches the description in each one of the boxes, and write their name in the box. A person can only put his name in one box per page.

Variations: Various charts can be made to accommodate the age group.

Geared Groups: Works well with groups of all ages.

Questions:

- What surprised you about this activity?
- How did this exercise prepare you for the rest of the program?
- How can this activity relate to the real world (i.e., work, school, etc.)?

#58: It's an Old Trick, but...

Materials: Paper, pencils

Number of Participants: Groups of 20 or more

Description: The leader of the activity should present a problem that is universal to the group. Have the participants either work individually or form groups of two to three people. Each unit should brainstorm as many solutions to the problem as possible within a specified amount of time, usually three to five minutes. Emphasize that no solution is too radical or not worthy of consideration. After the time is up, let each unit presents their solution(s) to the large group for review.

Variations: Groups from different areas within the organization can crossover and provide solutions to problems in different areas.

Geared Groups: Works well with groups of all ages.

Questions:

- Can an enhancement/improvement be made to one of the solutions provided?
- Was there a particularly creative approach in searching for possible solutions?
- How can this activity relate to the real world?

#59: Line Up

Materials: Blindfolds

Number of Participants: Seven or more; also works very well with large groups

Description: Explain that no talking or lip-synching is allowed during this exercise. Their task is to line themselves up in order according to their date of birth. Do not tell them which end is January and which is December—make them decide. Do not allow writing, but encourage other forms of communication, mainly body language. Direct them to line-up perpendicular to a wall. Allow them to define the perpendicular direction. Some will line up with their bodies perpendicular to the wall, while other groups will form the entire group line perpendicular to the wall.

Variations: Have them line up according to different criteria (i.e., age, alphabetically by middle names, hometowns, etc.). This is a good way to have the participants group up for future activities as well, by lining up this way and then counting off.

Geared Groups: Works well with those of college age and older.

Questions:

- What obstacles did you have to overcome?
- Looking back, is there another method that may have made this activity easier to complete?
- Did someone take a leadership role in this activity? Did this help contribute to the success? If so, would you have succeeded otherwise?
- Was there anything that hindered the successful completion of the activity?

#60: Magnet

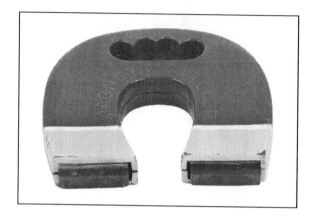

Materials: Pre-made cards illustrating themes, as well as "support" cards for each of the themes

Number of Participants: Medium to large size groups

Description: Deal cards facedown, one to each player. Instruct participants to seek out four (or any other number) people who have cards that are most similar to the one they have received. Instruct each group to think of a name and a sound for themselves based on their cards. Have them explain their choices.

Variations: Instead of dealing the cards, have individuals choose their card.

Geared Groups: Works well with groups of all ages.

Questions:

- How did the group ensure that their theme show through both the group name and sound?

- If participants have chosen their own cards: Does the theme you chose reflect your personality?

#61: Meet Your Neighbors

Materials: Handouts with boxes containing various categories, pencils

Number of Participants: Large groups of 40 to 70 participants can meet many others in their group, or medium-size groups

Description: Each participant receives a sheet of paper divided into boxes with different categories (e.g., "Name a time when you did something dangerous," or "Have you been to Europe?"). Each person can then tape this paper to himself and set off in search of individuals who can fulfill the requirements of the boxes.

Geared Groups: This activity works well for people of all ages. It also works great with those participants who want to get to know each other better.

Questions:

- Did you have any pre-existing assumptions about people before you met them?

- Were you surprised by some of the responses you read?

- What does this exercise suggest about the people with whom you interact with each day?

- How did the things that you were able to sign under contribute to who you are today and how you react in certain situations?

#62: Name Echo

Materials: None

Number of Participants: Medium to large size groups

Description: Arrange participants in a circle. Have the first person say their name and make up a motion or sound. When the second person says his name and sound, and it is repeated by the group, he then repeats the first participant's name and action as well. This continues around the circle until each person has had a chance to make up a movement, remembering to repeat the actions of all of those who have presented already.

Geared Groups: Groups who do not know each other well, and any age group.

Questions:

- Did this help you remember the names of the members of your group?
- What did the action that each person performed tell you about them? Did you learn things about your fellow participants that you did not previously know?
- Do you think this energizing activity helped get you motivated for the rest of the day?

#63: Negotiation

Materials: Pre-made cards illustrating themes, as well as support cards for each of the themes

Number of Participants: Medium to large-size groups

Description: Form groups of four to five people and deal 15 cards to each group. Have the groups discuss their cards and pick three that represent the group's overall personality. Have them present their explanations to the large group.

Variations: Split participants into groups based on their personality. Separate each color into its own group, put one of each personality type in each group, etc.

Geared Groups: Works well for groups of all ages.

Questions:

- How did the group's personalities reflect the theme your group decided on?
- Did anyone's personality type get compromised? Could you have picked a theme that represented all of the personalities?
- How did you see your personality type show while deciding on your theme(s)?

#64: Astrology

Materials: None (although an astrological information chart may be helpful)

Number of Participants: Works well with medium to large group

Description: Form groups based upon astrological signs. Each subgroup develops a list of commonalities among its members. Allow each group to determine what types of qualities are common to the individuals and which should be brought forward for presentation to the group as a whole.

Variations: Split participants into subgroups based on the time of day or day of the week they were born.

Geared Groups: Works well for groups of all ages.

Questions:

- Did some subgroups hold back certain qualities?
- Were there Variations among certain qualities that were determined to be important to each subgroup? Which qualities?
- Were all the qualities positive or did some subgroups present negative qualities as well?

#65: Team Branding

Materials: Markers, paper

Number of Participants: Works well with any size group, but works best with groups of 30 or more

Description: Divide the participants into teams of at least six members. Have each team come up with their own slogan or symbol (i.e., Block I). It is also imperative that each team be divided into smaller subgroups (of three to seven members), so the dominant members of the group cannot stifle the ideas of less dominant members who may have very different interpretations of the makeup of their team or how the team could be defined. After getting input from the subgroups and deciding on a team brand, each team should present their idea to the other teams.

Geared Groups: Works well for college students.

Questions:

- What comes to mind when you think of Starbucks? What is Starbucks selling that makes it unique when compared to other coffee shops?

   Possible answers might include: quality coffee, trends, cool and hip atmosphere, style. Similar questions can be asked about other companies, particularly ones that would be familiar to the team or group.

- What comes to mind when you think of the team or group?

- What makes your team/group unique when compared to similar teams/groups?

#66: The Joy of Four

Materials: Small sheets of paper with information written on them, e.g., team mascot names, team colors, grades in school (some cards are the same), small blank sheets of paper

Number of Participants: Any size group, as long as several groups of four can be made

Description: Each individual is given a sheet of paper. They are then instructed to find their group based upon the information on their piece of paper. Individuals, including those who have blank cards, should work to find three other people who are holding the same card.

Geared Groups: Works well for any age group.

Variations: This game can also be played as the Joy of Six.

Questions:

• How did it feel when you found someone with the same message?

• How does it feel to be accepted into a group or team? Does it make you feel better knowing you now have several new friends?

• How would you have felt if you were the only one to receive a blank piece of paper?

• Does it ever happen at school or work that someone is not chosen or put in a group? How does that person probably feel? Is it always intentional?

• What are things we can do to include others "in the loop"?

• What lessons does this have for team building?

#67: To Tell the Truth

Materials: Chairs for each participant

Number of Participants: At least 10, but the larger the group, the better

Description: Place the chairs in a circle and have everyone sit down. Have participants take turns asking yes/no questions (i.e., "Do you have a cat?") People must decide for themselves if the answer is yes or no. If the answer is no, they remain seated, but if the answer is yes, they move over one seat to the right. This will cause some people to be piled on other people's laps and is a lot of fun. Make sure that the content of the questions asked are clean and appropriate. In the event that the person on the bottom or middle of a pile is a "yes" and someone on his lap is a "no", everyone on top of the "yes" lap must move with him.

Variations: Play around by removing empty chairs or changing the distance or direction to travel per question. (i.e., move two seats to the left for "yes," one seat to the right for "no," etc.) You could also change this so a "yes" means everyone must get up and take a different seat, making sure that there is one chair fewer than there are people. The person without a seat must ask the next question.

Geared Groups: Works well for all ages and organizations.

Questions:

- Did this activity help you loosen up for the rest of the day?
- How did this activity help you prepare you for the activities to come?
- Did this activity give you the chance to get to know your fellow participants better? Was personal space an issue?

#68: Magnetism

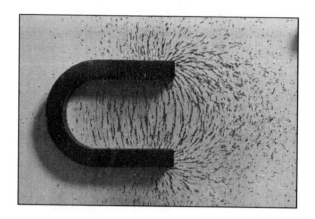

Materials: 3" x 5" index cards with pairs of words that attract each other (i.e., bees-honey)

Number of Participants: Medium to large size groups

Description: Each participant picks up a card upon entering the room. When the entire group is present, explain what is meant by a match and that each person should begin searching the group for their match. Once they locate that person, they introduce themselves.

Variations: Change the words from things that attract to things that are opposite or repel.

Geared Groups: Works well for groups high-school-age or older.

Questions:

- Did the activity allow you to meet someone new?
- Was there confusion over which words were paired (attractive) to others?
- Did the members of the group easily find their match?

#69: Are You One?

Materials: A list of questions including characteristic identifiers

Number of Participants: Medium to large size group

Description: Line up all the participants on one side of the room. Ask a series of defining questions such as, "Do you have blue eyes?" Everyone who answers "yes" crosses over to the other side of the room. Everyone who answers "no" stays where they are. Through a series of questions, the group ebbs and flows from side to side in the room. Allow time for the group to observe which members are moving with the answer to each question.

Variations: Limit the questions to work or life experiences only.

Geared Groups: Works well for any age group.

Questions:

- Were members able to learn something new about their co-workers?
- Did the exercise make the differences and similarities between group members more evident?
- Did any question(s) place a vast majority of the group on one side or the other?

#70: The Postman

Materials: Pad of Post-it® notes per participant, pieces of paper with the first name of one participant per page written on it, tape

Number of Participants: Any number

Description: Assemble the group and have them spend about five minutes introducing themselves to as many of the other members of the group using only their first name. Using the Post-it® notes each member should write down a characteristic about the other person that will enable them to better remember their name. Tape the first names on the walls and have the members of the group post their identifying characteristics under the appropriate name. Allow participants latitude with the identifying characteristics knowing that they will be posted for all to see.

Variations: Require the person writing the identifying characteristic to sign the Post-it® note.

Geared Groups: Works well for high-school-age groups or older.

Questions:

- Did people generally use some physical characteristic such as height or hair color to identify?

- Was anyone surprised by what others used to identify them? Did that generate any discussion or offense?

- Did the group members have fun with this exercise?

#71: Letter by Letter

Materials: 3" x 5" index cards with various words containing four letters written on them, pencils

Number of Participants: Any number

Description: Have the words printed in all capital letters on the index cards (one four-letter word per card). Have each member of the group take a card and work independently to develop four descriptive terms for the individual's work style using the four letters of the word printed on the card. Each person shares his four terms with the group.

Variations: Design the words so that many letters of the alphabet are used and duplications are minimized.

Geared Groups: Works well for any age group.

Questions:

- Did the group learn something new about the other members?
- Was this a simple exercise for most of the group members?
- Did some participants choose to create words that were descriptive of themselves?
- Was anyone restricted by the letters of their word?

#72: Time Traveler

Materials: Paper, pencils

Number of Participants: Any number

Description: Let each member choose a time period to which they would like to travel. Explain the positives and negatives of being a part of the selected time period. How were things different during this period? How were things the same? Each person in the group shares his selection with the larger group.

Variations: Limit the time travel to a particular event.

Geared Groups: Works well for any age group.

Questions:

- What motives did the person have for choosing a specific period of time?
- Were all the choices to travel to the past or did some people choose to go into the future?
- Did anyone wish not to time travel at all?

#73: Am I Famous?

Materials: 3" x 5" index cards with the names of famous people written on them, masking tape

Number of Participants: Medium to large size groups

Description: Place the index cards face down on a table. As the members of the group enter the room, tape one card to their back being careful not to let the person see the name on the card. Members of the group may then go around the room asking yes/no questions in an attempt to identify the name on their card. Once each member has identified his name, he must remain available to answer questions from other members.

Variations: Use names of an identified demographic group such as U. S. Presidents or international heads of countries.

Geared Groups: Works well for high-school-age groups or older.

Questions:

- Did the exercise provide the amount of mixing among the members that was expected?
- Did the names provide a challenge level that was appropriate for the group–difficult enough to encourage interaction among the members, but not so difficult as to cause frustration?

#74: They Say It's Your Birthday

Materials: None

Number of Participants: Medium to large size groups

Description: Give the group the direction that you would like everyone to line up on one side of the room in chronological order according to their birthdays. Allow the group to determine how the task is to be completed, but don't allow them to take too long to accomplish the job. Following completion, ask for the feelings of the group members on how the process went. How could it have gone better? Worse?

Variations: Have the male members on one side and the female members on the other. Race to completion.

Geared Groups: Works well for any age group.

Questions:

- Through non-verbal actions, did the group learn something about its members that it did not already know?
- Were any members of the group reluctant about revealing their age?
- Did a leader emerge to take control of accomplishing the task?

#75: I'm With...

Materials: 3" x 5" index cards with the names of famous partners on each card, masking tape

Number of Participants: Any number

Description: On each card write the name of one member of a famous duo such as Dean Martin and Jerry Lewis. Each member of the group receives a card that gets taped to his back in such a way that he cannot read the card. Then, they proceed around the room asking yes/no questions of other people in an attempt to find their famous partner. Continue until people identify themselves and their famous partners.

Variations: Pair people up by giving them the same name and they have to find their match.

Geared Groups: Works well with any age group as long as the names are familiar to the group.

Questions:

- Was finding your partner an easily accomplished task?
- Were some of the members of the group not familiar with the names on the cards?
- Were distinctions in ages made evident through this activity?
- Did the group enjoy the interaction?

#76: Draft Choice

Materials: 3" x 5" index cards, pencils, masking tape

Number of Participants: Large groups

Description: Designate three to six individuals to act as the general manager of their team. A random draw is held to determine the order in which each team shall draft its "players." Each general manager selects one person by placing their name on an index card when their turn to draft comes up and that person joins the team. The order of the draft reverses with the completion of each round. On the second round, both members of the team have to agree upon a player to select and so on until all the members of the group have been selected on the team. Cards with the players' names are arranged on the wall near the general manager's seat for all to see. Each manager in consultation with his team members then shares the team's strategy of drafting its players.

Geared Groups: Works well with high-school-age groups or older.

Questions:

• How did the feelings of those drafted first differ from those who were drafted later?

• Did the dynamics of the selection change with the addition of each new player to the team?

• Did the exercise bring back memories of being the last person chosen when playing a kid's game?

5

Better Business

#77: Isn't That Special?

Materials: 11" x 17" sheets of paper, colored markers

Number of Participants: Any number

Description: Individuals or small groups from working groups within the organization design and produce a poster displaying their most significant contribution(s) to the organization over the last year. Following completion, each individual or group presents their special accomplishments to the group. Allow time for comments on the design and content, as well as questions as to why something was considered significant.

Variations: Ask that each poster list the three top accomplishments for the organization. Compare and contrast the content between the groups.

Geared Groups: Almost any age group that has a common goal.

Questions:

- What did the group learn about its sub-units or individuals in this exercise?
- Which was more important: the design or the content?
- Were there commonalities or differences?

#78: Let's Do It Again

Materials: Paper, pencils

Number of Participants: Any number, formed into small groups according to function within the organization

Description: Each group should be given several sheets of paper and pencils. The group is instructed to design a model of review and replacement for the programs and services of the organization. What programs need to be reviewed and how frequently should the reviews take place? Each model should include specifics such as the who, what, when and why of the program review. The groups present their plans to the organization as a whole with time for questions and comments.

Geared Groups: Almost any age group that has a common goal.

Variations: Form groups mixed with participants from different areas within the organization.

Questions:

- Were the differences between the groups evident?
- Was the process divisive or did it bring people closer?
- Did the final plan represent elements from all the groups or did one dominate?

#79: The Rollercoaster

Materials: Paper, pencils

Number of Participants: Any number

Description: Working individually, each member of the group writes the three "highest" points and the three "lowest" points in his life. After an appropriate development time the group reconvenes and each person is asked to share his list with the group.

Geared Groups: Almost any age group, but works best with high school age participants and older.

Variations: Limit the highs and lows to time within the organization or a specific time frame such as their time in high school.

Questions:

- What did the group learn about its members in this exercise?
- How willing were members to openly share their lists?
- Were there more commonalities or differences?

#80: Taking Stock

Materials: Paper, pencils

Number of Participants: Any number

Description: Each person should be given a sheet of paper and a pencil. Working individually, each participant creates two columns: one for a list of positive accomplishments in his overall performance within the organization and one for a list of negative factors. Following a brief period of development, the individuals are paired to review their lists. Honesty is the key in the development of the lists.

Geared Groups: Almost any age group, but works best with high school age participants and older.

Variations: Personalize by asking for lists of items that contribute to the personal well-being of each participant.

Questions:

- What did the group learn about its members in this exercise?
- Were members willing to openly share their lists?
- Were there more commonalities or differences?

#81: Mother Hen

Materials: Paper, pencils

Number of Participants: Small to medium size groups

Description: Have the participants list areas that are still in need of development and nurturing to reach their fullest potential. Each area should include the type and extent of "mothering" needed from the organization to proceed to fruition. The assistance needed should include both internal and external conditions as well as those things within and outside of the control of the organization.

Variations: Have the group determine the priorities of the top three to five items that need nurturing. Each individual then lists how he can assist in providing the needed development conditions.

Geared Groups: Works well with high school groups or older

Questions:

- Were items listed geared more toward meeting the needs of the organization or more toward the individual?

- How many of the conditions needed were under the direct control of the organization?

- Did your group respond with creative and clever ways of contributing to the solutions and conditions?

#82: State of the Union

Materials: Paper, pencils

Number of Participants: Works well with small groups made up of leadership positions

Description: Each participant is designated as the president of the company or head of the organization/unit. They are asked to prepare a three to five minute "state of the union" address to other members of the group. Allow latitude in the preparation in order to give individuals the ability to determine their own direction and priorities.

Variations: Limit the speech to one aspect of the organization such as personnel or finances.

Geared Groups: Works well with "business" groups.

Questions:

- Where did the individuals place their priorities?
- Were the speeches more broadly based on the state of the organization or did they narrow in on one or two aspects of the organization?
- Were there any consistent themes that went across individuals?

#83: The Dead Zone

Materials: Paper, pencils

Number of Participants: Medium to large size groups

Description: Divide the group into pairs who will work independently of each other. Working alone each person lists those items that can "kill" a project, program or service. These items should include both internal and external influences as well as those that are within and outside of the control of the organization.

Variations: Divide the larger group based upon sub-units within the organization.

Geared Groups: Works well with high-school-age participants and older.

Questions:

- How did the various "killing" items differ between individuals?
- Was there any consistency or agreement on a single item?
- Were most of the items listed under the control of the organization or did most come from outside the realm of control for the organization?

#84: How Am I Doing?

Materials: Paper, pencil

Number of Participants: Smaller groups

Description: Divide the group into smaller units of three to four participants. Have each unit brainstorm ideas on providing feedback and recognition to employees of the organization. Reconvene the group and have each unit share their three best ideas. Encourage discussion and feedback from the entire group on each idea.

Variations: Divide the smaller units according to age or working subgroups within the organization.

Geared Groups: Works well with high-school-age participants and older.

Questions:

- What new information did the group discover about the subgroups?
- Did the responses differ from group to group or were they consistent across the board?
- How was the feedback from the larger group received and processed by the sub-group?

#85: Famous Quotes

Materials: Paper, pencils, list of selected quotes

Number of Participants: Small to medium size groups

Description: Distribute a list of selected quotes to all members of the group. Each member is asked to select a quote that best describes him or his work style. Members are then individually asked to explain how the selected quote describes him or his work style. Allow for duplications of quotes and interaction between the group and the individual.

Variations: Allow the individuals to present their own favorite quote without supplying a list.

Geared Groups: Works well with high-school-age participants and older.

Questions:

- Were selections made based on the actual quote or an affinity for the author?
- Did one quote dominate the selection?
- Did the selection stimulate an exchange between the members of the group and the individual?

#86: A Clean Sweep

Materials: Large sheets of Post-it® paper, markers

Number of Participants: Medium to large groups

Description: Divide the larger group into subgroups of three to four people. Have the smaller groups brainstorm for projects that have remained unfinished within the organization and then discuss the impediments that are preventing them from being completed. Allow a sufficient amount of time for full development of the list of unfinished work. Post the sheets on the wall, eliminate the duplications, and have the group analyze ways to move these projects to fruition. The length of time needed for this may be considerable.

Variations: Restrict the items to changes in policy or a similarly smaller arena for discussion.

Geared Groups: Works well for groups high school age or older.

Questions:

- Did areas identified for resolution address organizational issues or were they specific to a smaller area within the overall unit?

- Was the number of items developed large or small?

- Were items listed under the control of the organization or were outside factors beyond the organization's control holding the progress in limbo?

#87: It's the Law

Materials: Paper, pencils

Number of Participants: Small groups

Description: Working independently, each member of the group is asked to develop a plan to address the degree of professional latitude that is appropriate for his subordinates. No one is given any direction as to how many, what type, or what level of employees this policy should apply to, only that the subordinates are professional, full-time employees. Every member shares his plan with the larger group. Encourage discussion and a complete exchange of ideas.

Variations: Give each person a different level or classification of employees for which to develop his plan.

Geared Groups: Works well for college-age or older executive-type groups.

Questions:

- Did one plan emerge as applicable for all levels and types of employees?
- Did the members attempt to address a plan for only those employees under their supervision or did they go across the board of the organization?
- Did anyone suggest that this issue should be dealt with on a case-by-case basis?

#88: My Toolbox

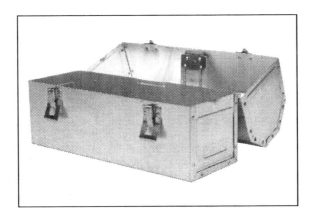

Materials: Paper, pencil

Number of Participants: Small to medium size groups

Description: Working independently, each member of the group list the "tools" he has available to do his job. These tools should include most physical and mental items that are used or needed to complete a job to the best of each member's ability. Each person should differentiate between what he currently has in his toolbox and what he needs to add or subtract from his toolbox.

Variations: Have each person prioritize the tools available and where on the list any new tools would fit.

Geared Groups: Works well for high school age group or older.

Questions:

- Were members able to easily describe all of the tools available to them in relation to their job?

- Did more tools deal with the physical side of their jobs or with the mental/ emotional side?

- Were the tools suggested to be added to the toolboxes something the organization could reasonably provide?

#89: On Second Thought

Materials: Large sheets of Post-it® paper, markers

Number of Participants: Medium size groups

Description: Divide the group into work- or task-related subgroups. Pose the following question to each subgroup: If they could start over again in their professional area, how would they do things differently? The "new" plan they create can include programs recycled from the past, completely new programs, and anything in between. Provide subtle parameters without restricting the ability to completely reshape the attitude, content, and delivery of the program. Each subgroup should write down their suggestions/ideas, then share their "new" plan with the larger group. Encourage discussion and explanation for the changes.

Variations: Have each subgroup redesign the entire organization.

Geared Groups: Works well for high-school-age groups or older.

Questions:

- Were members able to envision a completely different world or did their changes concentrate on minor alterations to the operation?
- Was there any nostalgia for long-standing programs and services?
- Did a particular subgroup represent a radical approach to redesigning their professional area that you would be interested in hearing more information on?

#90: What's Your Role?

Materials: List of traditional roles within the organization, paper, pencil

Number of Participants: Smaller groups

Description: Working independently, each member of the group chooses one of the traditional roles from the list provided and develops what he believes to be the behaviors expected from that role. Reconvene the group and have each member share his expected behaviors for his chosen role. Encourage dialog between the group and the presenter regarding the expected behaviors.

Variations: Assign roles for development that are different than those already performed by the individual.

Geared Groups: Works well with high-school-age and older groups.

Questions:

- Did most of the roles selected center around being the person in charge or the boss?
- Were interpretations of the expected behaviors of a particular role dramatically different from individual to individual?
- Were different members of the group able to share and defend their set of expected behaviors without fear of other's opinions?

#91: Waiting for Clearance

Materials: Paper, pencils

Number of Participants: Small to medium size groups

Description: Ask each member of the group to write down on paper two things that they have been procrastinating about in their life. Have them also list the reasons for delaying the completion of these items. Each member shares at least one of their items with the group. Encourage discussion and exchange of ideas between the individual and the group.

Variations: Limit the items to personal, non-work related situations.

Geared Groups: Works well for high-school-age groups or older.

Questions:

- Did people generally list personal or work-related items?
- Were the factors causing the delay of completion under the control of the individual?
- Were participants easily willing to share the fact that they procrastinate on certain items in their lives?

#92: That Will Never Fly

Materials: 3" x 5" index cards, pencils

Number of Participants: Small to medium size groups

Description: Ask each member of the group to write on a card one or two ideas to improve the performance of the organization that they feel might be too radical to implement in reality. Emphasize that there are no restrictions on the size or scope of any idea and the purpose of the exercise is "think outside the box." Individual members share their ideas with the group. No idea can be rejected without a thorough review by the group. Encourage discussion and modifications from the group on any individual idea proposed.

Geared Groups: Works well for any age group.

Questions:

- Were any usable ideas generated during this exercise?

- What was the most outlandish idea proposed and could it be feasible 10 years from now?

- Did position in the organization play a role in whether or not an idea was considered possible?

#93: We Do It Best

Materials: Paper, pencil

Number of Participants: Any number

Description: Each member of the group lists on his paper one or two items that they believe their organization does better than any other organization. Do not limit the items to programs or services, but rather allow the members to include even the most minute courtesy (i.e., greeting everyone with a smile) to more prominent statements (i.e., providing the best value for the money spent). Ask each presenter to explain why they believed this item was what the organization prides itself on

Variations: Ask the members to provide those things that the organization does worse than anyone else.

Geared Groups: Works well for high-school-age groups and older.

Questions:

- Was there an item mentioned more frequently than any other?
- Did those members higher up in the organization choose items that were distinctly different from those of lower level employees?
- Did the explanations of why items were chosen change anyone else's mind in the group regarding that item?

#94: That's the Ticket

Materials: Paper, pencils

Number of Participants: Larger groups

Description: Divide the larger group into subgroups based upon common criteria. It works the best if these subgroups either work together or interact regularly working toward a common goal. Each subgroup is given the task of listing what their group expects to get out of attending this function. The statement(s) must be the consensus of all of the members of the subgroup. The subgroup presents to the larger group in an effort to develop a common expectation for the larger group before proceeding further with the function.

Variations: If the group is small, use individual responses rather than those of a subgroup.

Geared Groups: Works well for any age group.

Questions:

- Was there open and free dialog in the subgroups when forming the expectations?
- Was the group able to reach a consensus and move on?
- Did expectations differ according to the level of the members of the subgroup?

#95: Halloween

Materials: Oversized clothing, glasses, masks, wigs, etc.

Number of Participants: Small groups

Description: Using the materials provided, each member of the group puts on a disguise. Following a sufficient amount of preparatory time, each member presents their disguise to the group. Discussion should center around why disguises are sometimes necessary in the workplace and when their use is appropriate. Reasons for the use of these devices should follow. Encourage discussion between the presenting person and the group.

Variations: If the group is larger, use drawings of a disguise in place of the actual disguise.

Geared Groups: Works well for any age group.

Questions:

- Was the group able to make the connection between the physical disguises of the exercise with the more subtle disguises used in the workplace?
- Was the exercise fun for the group?
- Did the group understand the importance and use of disguises when the exercise was completed?

#96: Shape Up

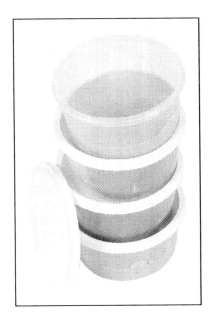

Materials: One stick of modeling clay per person

Number of Participants: Smaller groups

Description: Set aside 10 to 15 minutes of time and allow each member of the group to produce a sculpture that represents themselves as part of the larger group. Give as little direction as possible in order to permit the members to take the task in any direction they feel appropriate. Each individual shares his sculpture and an explanation with the larger group.

Variations: Have groups of two to three individuals decide on the shape and scope of the sculpture.

Geared Groups: Works well for any age group.

Questions:

- Were the members of the group creative in the interpretation of the task?
- How many members continued to request for more direction and parameters even after you told them the sculpture was completely up to them and their imagination?
- Did any of the members want to keep their sculpture following the exercise?

#97: Upon Further Review

Materials: Paper, pencil

Number of Participants: Medium to large groups

Description: Have each member of the group write down on a piece of paper an aspect of the organization that needs additional scrutiny. Explain that nothing within the organization is off limits. Programs, services, personnel, or policies are just a few of the examples of areas that could be included. Providing parameters or leaving it to the discretion of the individual members is left to be decided by the facilitator. Members share their areas for scrutiny with the larger group. An open and honest exchange of reasons for the choice is the goal of the exercise.

Variations: Limit the review suggestions to only one aspect such as policies or programs.

Geared Groups: Works well for high-school-age groups or older.

Questions:

- Did any member concentrate his ideas for review to one area such as programs more than another?

- Did the explanations for the selections stimulate discussions between the member and the remaining members of the group?

- Was anyone offended or did anyone become defensive over another member's selection?

#98: Who? Me?

Materials: Sheets of paper, pencils, timer if you are going to be strict with time, several suggestions for questions

Number of Participants: Small to medium size groups

Description: Give each person a sheet of paper and a pencil. Ask them to write down a maximum of four questions that they would ask someone they just met in an atypical situation. Tell them to steer away from the most obvious questions. Then, have the participants pair off and ask each other the questions they wrote down. After 10 minutes, ask each participant to stand up and say his name aloud. Then, the person he was paired with tells the group something he found out about the person standing. Allow as many facts to be stated as time permits

Geared Groups: Works with all ages.

Questions:

- How did this get you ready for the rest of the day?
- Did you learn anything about the personalities of your fellow participants through this activity?

#99: Wake-Up Call

Materials: Post-it® sheets for the wall, markers

Number of Participants: Medium to large groups

Description: Break the larger group into subgroups of four to six people. The subgroup should be made up of members from different areas within the larger group if there are organizational divisions within the group. Have each subgroup work for 15 to 20 minutes developing "wake-up calls" the organization has received during the past year. These can be internally or externally generated and must be explained as to their source, the salient issue, and a solution or reaction proposed from the organization. Each subgroup then shares their wake-up calls with the larger group.

Variations: Form the subgroups around the natural area divisions within the organization.

Geared Groups: Works well for high-school-age groups or older.

Questions:

- Were any new ideas for the organization generated by this exercise?
- Did the exercise challenge people to produce solutions to the wake-up calls?
- Did the wake-up calls concentrate in one part of the organizational operation?

#100: Designing Ways

Materials: T-shirts with black and white line designs, colored permanent markers for use on cloth

Number of Participants: Smaller groups

Description: For your next organizational function where team members need to be identified by wearing a certain t-shirt, provide each member of the group with a t-shirt that bears only a black and white line drawing of the design for the event. Allow each person to customize his t-shirt design through the use of the colored permanent markers. Display the "designs" on the wall during the remainder of the meeting.

Variations: Have pairs of individuals design the shirts for their partners.

Geared Groups: Works well for any age group.

Questions:

- Did the members of the group utilize the colored markers to complete the existing design?
- Did anyone embellish their design by adding something outside of the original line design?
- Would your organization feel comfortable in having your staff seen at the proposed event wearing these designs?

#101: On a Mission

Materials: Post-it® sheets for the walls, pencils

Number of Participants: Smaller groups

Description: Either have the group work as individuals or divide the larger group into subgroups of no more than three people. Everyone is asked to take 15 minute and develop a mission statement for the organization. A limited amount of guidance is suggested (i.e., length and purpose) to allow the participants the latitude to include in their mission statement everything they feel is appropriate. All the statements are discussed with the individual or group representative explaining the rationale behind their mission statement. Consensus is reached through a free and open exchange of ideas.

Variations: Provide the mission statement and ask the group members to provide goal statements to accompany it.

Geared Groups: Works well with high-school-age groups or older.

Questions:

• Was a consensus reached and an acceptable mission statement found?

• Did any subgroups or individuals withdraw from the process due to the exclusion of the elements of their suggested mission statement?

• Was the process easy or difficult?

About the Authors

Gary Miller, Ph.D., is currently the associate director of the division of campus recreation at the University of Illinois at Urbana-Champaign, a position he has held since 1990. His responsibilities include research; field/building maintenance and construction; and technology. He has worked in the field of recreational sports for almost three decades at universities in California, Michigan, and Illinois. He holds degrees in business administration and recreation from the University of Illinois and in physical education from the University of Southern California. A prolific writer and a highly sought-after speaker at professional meetings across the United States, Dr. Miller is widely respected for his ability to understand and apply business concepts to his field.

Heather Horn is serving in her sixth year as a human resources specialist in the division of campus recreation at the University of Illinois at Urbana-Champaign. In addition to human resources, she has managed the ActiveLEAD (leadership) program, led a climbing tower as a certified climber, emceed multiple events, and conducted a professional conference as a graduate student. Heather, who coaches high school and club teams, played on the varsity volleyball team for the University of Illinois at Urbana-Champaign, where she earned her bachelor's degree in speech communications and received her masters at the Institute of Labor & Industrial Relations.